T0208271

Lyrics of Life

Tammy Sexton

authorHOUSE®

AuthorHouse™
1663 Liberty Drive
Bloomington, IN 47403
www.authorhouse.com
Phone: 1 (800) 839-8640

Published by AuthorHouse 07/10/2019

ISBN: 978-1-7283-1845-5 (sc)
ISBN: 978-1-7283-1846-2 (e)

Library of Congress Control Number: 2019909031

Print information available on the last page.

This book is printed on acid-free paper.

All About Mending

Healing hands, loving touch
Giving what they need so much
Caring heart, mindful thought
Remembering skills we've been taught
Having empathy for how they feel
Providing comfort for those who are ill
Showing that we truly care
Letting them know we'll be there
Teaching others, easing pain
A rewarding career with much to gain
A nurse's job, all about mending
A nurse's job, never ending

Just the Little Things

It's the little things
That matter so much
A simple smile
Or a loving touch
A kind word spoken
A helpful deed
Giving of yourself,
No harboring greed
A promise kept
A phone call made
Someone was lonely
So you stayed
A friendship gained
A sin forgiven
All others gave up
But you were driven
Just the little things
That say you care
We all should do
No matter where

Happiness

When happiness spreads
Flowers will bloom
Sun will shine brightly
Giving sadness no room
So put on a smile
And help others smile too
And happiness will spread
And find its way back to you

My Shadow

I'm being followed I swear, but when I turn around,
there's nobody there
I see it at night right behind me when I walk
But it doesn't say a word, I don't think it can talk

Sometimes it's long and stretchy, sometimes short and fat
And when I run it's right there with me, wherever I'm at
When I see it, it mocks everything I do
Look out when you're out there, it might follow you too

My Favorite Stuffed Animal

Always there for me in the dark of night
Bringing me comfort to make everything right
Going where I go without complaint
Soft and cuddly, cute and quaint
My favorite stuffed animal true to the end
You will always be my dearest friend

The Cat

Like a predator he hunches down
Quietly stalking his prey
Carefully listening, twitching an ear,
Hoping it will come his way
He waits, he watches, waiting for the time to be right
Just then he lunges, he's got it
He grips it tight
But wait a minute, he looks again
Oh, this can't be so
The cat's been fooled by those he loves
And a ball of yarn tied in a bow

A Mouse in My House

There is a mouse inside my house
And it is quite disturbing
It runs all around making mouse sounds
And it's getting so perturbing
I can't sleep at night
I'm filled with fright
What if it crawls into my bedding?
But what can I do?
I wish I knew
So I could stop this dreading
Set a trap or two?
Or the mousey glue?
I guess I'll have to be a little daring
Because my house, with a mouse, I'm not interested in sharing

Teddy Bear

Fuzzy and brown with never a frown
Arms made for hugging enduring a tugging
Keeping me near to chase away fears
I am your teddy bear

Spring is Here

Yellow sunshine, budding trees
Blooming flowers and a warm spring breeze
Buzzing bees and butterflies
Big soft clouds and warm blue skies
Cool green grass and nesting birds
Singing songs without words
Children laughing, playing near
All signs proving spring is here

The Butterfly

Floating on a summer breeze
Through the air, over the trees
I spread my wings and fly away
On a warm and sunny day
Graceful and quiet as I dance
You will give me a second glance
I am a butterfly sure and free
Take in my beauty, let me be

Grand Tetons

Majestic, they stand, soaring into the sky
As though to stand at attention
For the creator
A salute in his honor
Raising up to Heaven
Confident and strong
White caps atop their rugged peaks
Outlined in blue background
Enclosed by crisp mountain air
Breathtaking and stunning
Amazingly made
Exquisite and mighty
Yet I, a pebble next to them
Finds freedom here from city life
Invigorating spirit, refreshing renewal
Established in The Grand Teton mountain range

Break of Day

Morning dew, awakening sun
Little bunnies on the run
Gentle breeze, blue clear sky
Early birds take off and fly
Break of day, perfect time
To sit here now and write this rhyme

The Storm

Lightning flashing all around
Rain like rockets racing down
Thunder clashing rattling the room
No signs yet of stopping soon

Harder still the wind does blow
Whipping, whirling and howling so
The wet spring air comes raining in
I'm more scared now than I've ever been

But then as quickly as it came
Before I know it, it's gone again
Peaceful breeze without the howl
Thankfully, it's all over now

My Girl

Little girl of my very own
I'll look one day and you'll be grown
A beautiful woman where my child once stood
With distant memories of childhood
So each day now I'll hold you dear
Watch you grow and keep you near
Cause soon I know you'll spread your wings
And fly on your own to do grown up things

The Night

In the darkness, still I lay
Waiting here for break of day
The night forever seems to last
As time ticks by, slowly past
Peaceful is, to hear the breaths
Of my sweet children while at rest
Slumbering angels in rooms nearby
Underneath the moonlit sky
I say a prayer for their safe sleep
And through the night, our souls to keep
Please wake us to the morning light
And keep us Jesus in your sight
Restless no more as I sigh
We finally agree, the night and I

Dancing In

Dancing in on angels' feet
A brand-new baby here to meet
Stole some starlight from the sky
To put a twinkle in her (his) eyes
Softly landed here on earth
And hid her (his) wings at her (his) birth
An angel blessing from above
Sent here to teach us about love

Being Mommy

Hearing pitter patter down the hall
Giggling and laughing through the wall
Playing tag, reading a book
Going on an adventure, mommy come take a look
Saying I love you, holding them tight
Knowing that being there is exactly right
Being a mommy is most important to me
And I promise to be the best I can be

My Son

As I look upon your child face
I realize one day
A grown man will be in your place
I see you so innocent and sweet
The child I've come to know
The man I'll someday meet
I'll hold you close my little one
As my boy grows into a man
No matter how big or small, you'll always be my son

Bugs

All those bugs and all those worms
Some say the dirt is full of germs
But I don't care cause I'm a boy
And sometimes bugs are my favorite toy
There are bugs that crawl and bugs that fly
Some bugs are quick and some bugs are sly
So, don't be surprised if you might find
Bugs in my pocket, one of every kind

Medicine Mommy

She says she means well but I'm not sure
I hope someday they'll find a cure
For my fever and my cold
This taking medicine is getting old
My eyes are red, my nose is runny
And all of this is not too funny
And here she comes once again
To give me more of that yucky medicine
Where she gets it from, I can't tell
But I know it has an awful smell
And the taste is even ten times worse
(I think she thinks she is a nurse)
Please hurry doctor, find a cure
Cause mommy says she means well but I'm not sure

Wake Up

Wake up little sleepy head it's time now to get out of bed
Time to greet the morning sun, begin the day and have some fun
Thank God for another day and for the blessings sent our way
And when the day ends again, tomorrow yet, another begins

My Two Front Teeth

I've lost them now and now they're gone
But mommy says it won't be long
The new ones will come, I have to wait
I hope that they will come in straight
My two front teeth right now are missing
And with each word I'm sort of hissing
For now, I have a gummy grin
I'll be so glad when they come in

Summer Break

Summer break is almost here
The time is coming oh so near
To play and swim and have some fun
Under the beautiful summer sun
Then each day I'll get to sleep in
And wake in the morning with a great big grin
Cause I know I won't hear school bells today
And all day long I'll get to play

Soccer

Kick that ball and run! Run! Run!
Playing soccer is so much fun
Find the goal and kick it in
Let's get some points so we can win

Baby Parts

Baby feet, so very sweet
Baby hands, just as God planned
Baby eyes, so innocent and wise
Baby hair, some are bare
Baby cheeks, squeeze and squeak

The Treasure Box

Gee, I wonder what could be in that treasure box so shiny!
Mommy says I get to find out if I'm not too whiny
Could there be a matchbox car or maybe a toy gun?
Mommy says "could be" but only if I walk quietly and do not run
Maybe there's a basketball, a tractor or a funny elf
"Maybe" mommy says but I won't know if I
don't keep my hands to myself
Maybe there's a bat and glove or even a mysterious rock slate
Maybe I'll know later, right now I have to clean my plate
I hope there will be some stickers, a frisbee or a castle
But mommy says I better not give the teacher any hassle
With all these rules that mommy makes how's a boy to play?
I'm not real sure if I will know what's in that treasure box today

Gymnastics

Whirl, twirl, flip and spin
Up to the sky and down again
Hang up on a trapeze bar
Please be careful, the mats so far
Twist and wind through the air
Hold my breath and say a prayer
As I watch through the looking glass
You have so much fun in gymnastics class

Baby boy

What a miracle, what a joy
My beautiful, precious baby boy
You came from Heaven of this I'm sure
With a round little face and skin so pure
Big brown eyes and button nose
And all ten of your wiggly toes
You melt my heart; you make me smile
I want to hold you longer than a while
How wonderful a gift given to me
Thank you, God, for letting him be
You've brought me happiness my precious son
You make my life so much fun
Forever I'll love you through all time
I am so thankful you are mine

Baby Girl

I love her hands, I love her feet
Her tiny fingers are so sweet
Ten little fingers, ten little toes
I love to watch how much she grows
Her eyes of brown, her little chin
I love her corky little grin
She is a blessing from God above
I will shower her with lots of love
I love her laugh, I love her smile
I love to hold her for a while
She has put me in to a wonderful whirl
My beautiful precious baby girl

You Cared

Maybe you were there for them
To wipe a tear away
Perhaps you held them close
On a cold and rainy day
Thank you for the love you gave
And the tenderness you shared
Thank you for the time you spent
Showing that you cared

Days

Yesterday a memory
Today a brand-new day
Tomorrow seems uncertain
With the choices we must make

Time Flies

With each tick that passes by
We grow older, time does fly
So, fill your minutes with moments to last
For quickly they become
Moments of the past

Slow Down Time

How dare you time
To take from them
A sparkle of light
A bit of gem
That childlike wonder
Has left their eyes
And been replaced
With thoughts of wise
I know that growing
We all must do
But please slow down
I'm begging you

Is it Love

A kind soul
Has found his way
Into my life
But here to stay?
I don't know
where this will go
How it will end?
I do not know
In my story
Is there true love?
The kind the elderly
like to speak of?
So far till now
it's always sad
The love I longed
But never had

Atoms

We are but atoms
Bouncing around
Some connecting
Some falling down

Matters of the Heart

Matters of the heart
Confusing at best
How to choose one?
And leave all the rest
What if it's right?
What if it's wrong?
How will you know
You found the right one?

Heartbreak

I thought I loved you
You broke my heart
It never felt right
Right from the start
You built your walls
I had no chance
I wanted in
You held your stance
I needed more
You said no
And just like that
You let me go
Now I know
You didn't care
And this heartbreak
Just isn't fair

Will He

Will he love me?
I don't know
But in my heart
I pray so

Fondness

Two hearts grow even fonder
Each time they are away
And love brings them together
Forever in love to stay

My Love

Speak softly into my ear
Let me know you are near
Help me cast away my fears
Quiet as a gentle breeze
Rocking as if on the mild seas
No greater days than these
Hold me close the one I love
Steadfast and true like the dove
Let's show them what we're made of

Reunited

Dancing and gliding with the one that I love
We're together again at last here above
This time as angels, forever and free
Never to part again you see
I waited so patiently here at the gate
For her to arrive at our final date
Now we'll go on, two joined as one
Dancing and gliding under the sun

Separate Ways

A true found love
Never to part
With this ring
I give you my heart
Some years pass
The children grow older
The warmth and love
Now get colder
Sadness sets in
Days are spent crying
The two decide
They're done trying
And so, they go
Their separate ways
In hopes of finding
Better days

Angels in Our Midst

Angels walking in our midst
Some say they don't exist
Miracles happening every day
Don't believe it is what they say
But I know differently what is true
Angels are here with me and you
What about the little child
That seen you sad and made you smile?
Or the day you felt all alone
And your sister called you on the phone
You thought your heart would never mend
But there to help you was your best friend
And even the man from out of town
Helped you up when you fell down
The tiniest baby they said wouldn't survive
Twenty years later is healthy and alive
Even the ones we can't understand
Who had to go and take hold of God's hand
Were angels sent to us just for a while
To bless our journey and bring us smiles
The proof is around you just look and see
Angels are walking with you and me

Angel Messages

What messages have they that I must hear?
With angel wings rustling quietly near
In the night or in the day
What is it that they must say?
Messages of I love you, forgiveness and peace
Messages of I miss you and give what they need
Do to others as you want done to you
And to yourself and those around you always be true
Never ignore what you know should be right
And when you want to give up, give it one last strong fight
Stand for yourself, never give in
Make sure not to live a life full of sin
Life isn't fair, it wasn't meant to be
But you learn as you go and you'll soon be set free
So, listen intently when there's something you hear
You may find its angels wings rustling quietly near

Now Don't Cry About it

"Now don't cry about it"
Five words I'll never forget
In the most calm and loving voice
I have not heard again yet
I often wonder who it was
That cared about my tears
I wonder if he's here with me now
After all these years
Was it my guardian angel?
Or just an angel sent to me?
A spirit of a loved one?
Who looked down and saw my need?
In that moment
I knew there was more
Beyond this earth
It's what we're searching for

Having Faith

Having faith is hard to do
I hear no reply when I speak to you
Is it because I'm not listening well?
Or I just don't hear you? I cannot tell
I feel something I cannot see
Is it you? Here with me?

His Child

A child of light that's who I am
Sent into darkness to teach of the lamb
Though I may struggle and though I may fear
I sense you're with me, I know you're near
I must learn on my own
And come back to you once I am grown

Disconnected

Heart and mind continue at war
Even the vessel knows not what for
Like oil and water never to mix
Only a prayer can hope to fix

New Hope

Alone in the darkness
Afraid of the sun
Hiding in shadows
With nowhere to run
Pleading for help
With faraway eyes
Losing all hope
Softly she cries
Will anyone help her?
Will anyone see?
The demons she's fighting
She's trying to flee
Then out of nowhere
A twinkle of light
As her soul opens up
She's gaining her sight

Write

Sorrow and strife
Brought this pen to life
Something good from the bad
Happy from sad
Pick up your pen and let it begin
Free your soul of the dark
It starts with one spark

The Same

And in the end
We're all the same
Players of
This lifelong game

Conflicted

I am good but I am bad
I am happy but I am sad
I am light but I am dark
And trials here
Have left their mark
A constant battle
But I will win
I pray for salvation
Over sin

Always Stay Smiling

Always stay smiling
No matter the pain
Always keep dancing
Even in rain

A Far Away Place

Finding myself in a faraway place
Floating away weightless full of grace
Each breath I breathe deep in my soul
The only place I can feel whole
No pain, no sadness, no exhausting fear
Only solace found without crying one tear
The air is peaceful and warm and free
As it surrounds and encompasses me
Holds me close as a mother does a child
The atmosphere so gentle and mild
Not wanting to leave this warm embrace
Finding myself in a faraway place

So Sad

Why so sad do I have to be?
I have no reason, it's just me
My heart is breaking for nothing I guess
But that doesn't make the pain any less
You don't understand the pain that I hide
My soul feels cold and its dark inside
I push you away but I need a spark
Light my soul, lead me out of the dark

Alone

Alone but surrounded how can it be
In a world of so many
It only feels like me
I understand darkness
But I yearn for the light
In a world of so many
Will I ever win this fight?
My soul it feels broken
As I silently scream out
In a world of so many
There are so many doubts

Not my own

In this strange life not my own
I'll find myself
When my babies are grown
For now, it is what it has to be
For His own reasons
I cannot see

Busy Mind

I'm awake in the dark of night
Alone I sit with all that's not right
My mind is busy, it gets no rest
And I'm exhausted even at my best

The Light

Lost in a world
not seeming to care
Carrying burdens
Too heavy to bear
Yet in the darkness
Shines one light so bright
Along this great journey
Keep it in your sight

Not Me

Living in this strange place
I don't see me when I look at my face
Who am I and why am I here?
The past and the future are both so near
There is something else of that I'm sure
It's not an illness, there is no cure

A Hero

You show us courage
When we're afraid
We seem so weak
You seem so brave
You give all
To those in need
You do more
Then just a good deed
A protector, a defender
All the way to the end
On you and your honor
We know we can depend

Missing You

Sitting on the sand
Thousands of miles from home
I look at a picture of you
And wonder how much you've grown
At this moment I feel calm
Resting my eyes on your smile
I wish that I could come back home
And hold you for a while
Have you uttered your first word?
Have you taken your first step?
How many teeth are there?
Are you a big kid yet?
I miss you more than you could know
Over in this foreign land
But I promise to come home soon
And hold your little hand

Freedom

Freedom isn't free
It comes at quite a cost
Some of them come home
Some of them are lost
They stand together strong
Answering the call
Fighting for our freedom
All for one and one for all
They are our children
They are our brothers
They are our fathers
They are our mothers
So, when you say your prayers at night
Remember them
The ones who fight
And when you go about your way
Think of them
Throughout the day
We call them soldiers
Brave and strong and true
They are our heroes
Fighting for me and you

The Veteran

You judge my character by what you see
Without even taking a chance to know the real me
To you I'm a drifter with nothing to give
Lost in society with no place to live
But once I fought for the freedom you keep
So you can have your things and peace while you sleep
Now help me out I'm cold and alone
And just like you this place is my home

Love Will Bring You Back

Love will bring you home again
Back here with me the way it should have always been
Never again to be apart
Never again to have this ache in my heart

I Miss You

Time can mend that's what they say
But I'm never not thinking of you, not even one day
I see the pictures of when you were here
I hold them close to keep you near
I wish somehow, I could jump right in
And live that moment with you over again
I want to see you and hear your sweet voice
I want to touch your smiling face but now I don't have that choice
So, I close my eyes and see you there
With your smiling face and skin so fair
And I look through the memories I have stored within my heart
And keep you there safely never again to depart

Memories

Love builds memories and memories a bridge
To keep us close to those who've gone before
To help us go on through each day that goes by
Just when we think we can't take it anymore
As we mend, we remember all the days we had together
And keep the memories close at heart
So that we can continue to live and grow
And know we'll never really part

Missing You

I miss you today
I'll miss you tomorrow
My heart is grieving
Full of sorrow
But I know
I'll see you again
I'll just keep busy
Until then

Goodbye

Goodbye goes without saying
As you disappear without a word
And now the sound of my heart breaking
Is the only noise that can be heard

Vengeance

Why do you take them? To the Father I ask
These innocent children who leave way too fast
Another angel in Heaven is the only reply
Here in Heaven they don't have to cry
Why must they suffer and endure such pain?
From their misery is nothing to gain
Now my child you do not understand
I take them from their pain when I take them by the hand
I'm there with the children abused and afraid
I was there with the children who were so violently slayed
I am sad to see how the world is now, people with no conscience
who don't love and don't care
Are making my earth a world of despair
But those who caused even one child's pain
Will see in the end they had nothing to gain
What they have reaped will also be sewn
As I judge what they've done from here on my throne
The skies will grow dark as the clouds roll away
And vengeance will be mine on that last fateful day

Broken Heart

A broken heart in time will mend
I'll keep praying for you I'll be your friend
I'll help you pick up pieces
Of your shattered broken heart
And put them back together
Piece by piece and part by part
I can't say I know exactly how you feel
I have not lost a child, I pray I never will
But on that night, I heard your cry
As one of God's little angels
Learned that he could fly
Know that you are not alone
In your grieving and your tears
I'll keep you in my thoughts and prayers
Forever through the years

A Vapor in the Wind

Like a vapor in the wind
On a cold and misty night
You are there I know
Somewhere out of sight
I feel you standing near me
I hear your distant call
No one else is noticing
But you're here with us all
You've never really left us
In our hearts is where you are
And like the vapor in the wind
You're never very far

I See You

You're not really gone
I see you everyday
Riding on the gentle breeze
In the trees as they sway
On a child's angelic face
A bright and cheery smile
In a field full of flowers
Going on for miles
I see you on the mountaintop
Reaching for the sky
On each and every sunset
As the day turns into nigh
I hear the children's laughter
And I hear your laughter too
And I know that you are with us
In everything we do

If I Go

If I go
Please don't cry
It's see you later
Not goodbye
For I am there
Within your heart
In every memory
In every part
I'll always be there
Just whisper my name
And know I love you
Just the same

I am Happy

I am happy now and all is well
When I left you I was frail
But now I'm better than before
With no pain or sickness anymore
I've earned my wings with which to fly
I'm watching you from here up high
I'll check in every now and then
Until my love we're together again

Tiny Angel

Tiny angel we did not know
Why so soon did you have to go?

I had to spread my little wings
And fly to Heaven to do angel things

Tiny angel so sweet, so dear
We really wanted you to stay here

But even though you cannot see, I am there with you
When you think of me

Tiny angel he or she
why were you chosen not to be?

I'm playing with angels and someday you'll see
The reasons why I could not be

Tiny angel in Heaven above
Is someone there to give you my love?

God gives me his love and the angels do too
And each time they kiss me, they kiss me for you

I'm Sorry

I'm sorry that I had to go
The reasons why for now, untold
Please forgive the choice I made
If I was well I would have stayed
Don't be afraid I know you're strong
And it's okay to carry on
I loved you then, I love you now
I hope you find some peace somehow

Remember Me

What do you see groundkeepers?
What do you see?
When you're looking at this place where I rest
Are you even considering me?
I was once an infant so small and sweet
With velvet skin and tender cheeks
I grew into a young boy fast
And before I knew it my childhood was past
As a teen I enjoyed racing my cars, hanging out with friends
And wishing on a star
One summer day she came into my life
The wonderful woman I'm so glad to call my wife
Then she came to me and told me
a miracle was about to be
And I was there when she gave birth
And we became a family of three
For three years we lived happily
Filled with so much joy
Just teaching and loving our beautiful little boy
And then it wasn't long before
She said to me, soon we would be
A family of four
And oh, the joy I felt inside
My two boys fill me with pride
I can only tell you, I am so glad

To hear the two of them call me dad
And then one day we made the choice
To add to the family two more boys
The best of days was spent back then
Playing ball with family and friends
I was such a hard worker, I worked hard every day
And never did I let anything get in my way
I was still just a young man, at the age of 38
When God said it was time
That I enter through the gate
I really didn't want to leave and give up my earthly life
Because I am leaving behind four boys and a wife
I was fighting hard to stay but I knew they would understand
I was just so tired, so I held onto God's hand
Now the shell of who I used to be
Lies here beneath the ground
And for the ones I left behind, this is where peace is found
Don't sit down on my stone, don't neglect my bed
Don't think it doesn't matter
Consider me instead
Someday you will be here too
And will surely make this your plea
While my shell rests here in God's garden
Please take good care of me

-in loving memory
Fred Sanders
June 7th 1964 – April 25th 2003

Little Boy

The little boy

That brought them joy

Left them way too soon

With firework kisses

And only 4 birthday wishes

No way they could have known

A beaming smile

That shined for miles

On a redtop little boy

Laid to rest

While they do their best

To hold him in their hearts

Just in Case

Just in case I have to go

There are some things I want you to know

Just in case we don't get to say goodbye

I don't want you to be sad

You don't have to cry

Just in case I forgot to say it today

I love you more than you could know

In each and every way

Just in case forever seems too long

Just think of me here

And I'll never actually be gone

Gone

What becomes of us once we're gone?

Nothing left to carry on

Do we fly to Heaven and get our wings?

Or stay on earth to do other things?

Or do we wait for His return?

Once we've mastered what we learned?

Alone in the World

Alone in the world with no one to hold

A young baby cries out in the cold

He doesn't deserve this he can't understand

His life has meaning, and God has a plan

Then along comes a stranger

A hero untold

And this sweet baby's life

Begins to unfold

Grumpy Old Woman

I have stories to tell you if only you'd hear

I haven't much time my end is near

You think I'm boring with nothing to say

A grumpy old woman who has lost her way

But inside I'm much different than you'd ever know

So sit down and listen before I must go

The lines on my face you don't like to see

Are reflections of laughter between my children and me

My feeble old hands that aren't able to grasp

Caressed baby's soft cheeks many days in the past

My mind so forgetful always seeming to fade

Holds memories so dear of the life that I've made

My eyes that are aged and can just barely see

Remember beautiful sunsets and trees filled with green

My legs that won't hold me because of the strength they lack

Once sprinted like lightning when I was in track

Who I am now on the outside is so unfair

The young lady I once was is still there

So yes, I am an old woman, but I shouldn't be judged

Yes, I am an old woman who just wants to be loved

Connected

Souls connected so far apart
A friendship born right from the start
Wiser than all the souls I've met
A guardian angel I place my bet

Poetry

I'd rather write poetry
Then drift to sleep
I'd rather wear a smile
Then admit that I weep

Sick

I'm one with the bed
My body is lead
I can't seem to eat
Or even stand on my feet
The room is spinning
And I'm not winning
My head does ache
I need a break
Send me a cure
That works for sure

Who Are You

Wondering, wishing on a bright star
I've never met you but you know who you are
I hear them say "Daddy" and I want to too
Every man I see, I wonder if he's you
Do I have your blue eyes?
Do I have your chin?
What color is your hair?
Maybe we have the same grin
So many birthdays pass without knowing your name
No one there to call dad, it just isn't the same
Have you ever for half a second given any thought
To the child you created, and now you live without?
The emptiness inside only you can fill
I want to meet you someday
Someday still

My Dad

Greyish hair and bearded chin
Blue eyes like mine, we share the same grin
He likes music, and so do I
We're both chocolate lovers, a fact we can't deny
He's been thinking of me throughout the years
And finally meeting him has calmed my fears
The mystery man I sought out to find
Has proven to be one of a kind
And now I know my life's been blessed
He is my dad, he is the best

One of These Days

One of these days
I'll play tag with you
One of these days
I'll help you tie your shoe
One of these days
We'll toss a frisbee
One of these days
We'll sail the sea
One of these days
I'll give you a piggyback ride
One of these days
I'll take you to the park to slide
One of these days
I'll see you hit that homerun
One of these days
I promise we'll have fun
One of these days
I'll realize what I've missed
One of these days
You'll no longer be that child that wished
One of these days
How about today?

Riddle of the Clock

I have two hands
But no eyes to see
I can keep track of time
One of my numbers is 3

Castle

In my castle
Where I rest
I go to sleep
To feel my best

Tulip

I'm a pretty tulip
Standing alone
Next to an angel
Made of stone

Ping Pong

It's lots of fun to play this game
Ping and pong are its name

About the author

My name is Tammy Sexton. I have 2 (almost) adult children who inspire me every day to do the best I can do at whatever I'm doing. I grew up in a small farming town in Illinois. It's the kind of place where the people feel like family and even if you've never been there, you feel at home. I graduated in 1998 from Lakeland college in Mattoon, Illinois as a registered nurse. I have worked in many fields of nursing and have been writing poetry on the side for quite some time. During my career, and in my own life, I have witnessed the wide spectrum of emotions from joy of a brand-new baby to saying final goodbye's. I have captured these moments and found the poetic expression within them. I hope to reach something in everyone through my words.

Printed in the United States
By Bookmasters